D1224283

The Shell Book of
Practical and Decorative Ropework

Eric C Fry and Peter Wilson

David & Charles
Newton Abbot London
North Pomfret (Vt) Vancouver

British Library Cataloguing in Publication Data

Fry, Eric Cyril
  The Shell book of practical and decorative
  ropework.
    1. Knots and splices – Handbooks, manuals, etc.
    I. Title II. Wilson, Peter, b. 1938
    623.88'82   VM533

ISBN 0–7153–7615–2

© Eric C. Fry and Peter Wilson 1978

Typeset by HBM Typesetting Limited, Chorley
and printed in Great Britain
by the Alden Press, Oxford
for David & Charles (Publishers) Limited
Brunel House Newton Abbot Devon

Published in the United States of America
by David & Charles Inc
North Pomfret Vermont 05053 USA
Published in Canada
by Douglas David & Charles Limited
1875 Welch Street North Vancouver BC

Contents

Introduction

No matter how utilitarian a knot or piece of ropework may be, by long maritime tradition, it has to be seen to be good as well as being efficient. Hence the familiar turk's head that enhances the appearance of a tiller *and* gives the helmsman a firmer grip. There has, though, never been any question of decoration for its own sake because, whether it was an elaborate working knot or plaited cordage, each had its purpose and place in the overall scheme from tack knot and highly ornate sea-chest handles to tiddly mat.

The majority of the knots in this book are of the 'tiddly' kind. *Tit-ley* was the original word but, by the early 1900s, 'tiddly' had become the accepted seafaring expression for practically anything and everything which was 'fancy', 'out of the ordinary' or, by dictionary definition, 'simple perfection'. Whatever interpretation was given and in whatever context the really old-time sailorman used the original word may be left to the imagination but his son's best going-ashore clothes became his 'tiddly gear', he was said to look 'tiddly' when so dressed and even the pride of the Royal Navy, the Royal Sovereign, became the *Tiddly Quid.* (For the benefit of younger readers, a 'quid' was a colloquial term for a sovereign which was twenty shillings in old currency.)

Needless to say, the word had a strong association with rope, cordage and rigging of all descriptions, 'tiddly' or decorative ropework becoming not only a matter of personal pride but something that reflected the pride of the ship herself. While *The Shell Book of Knots and Ropework* dealt solely with working knots and splices, this book deals with the more elaborate, multi-strand, decorative work that is nevertheless always practical and will, we hope, stimulate interest in a thoroughly useful craft.

As before, each knot is illustrated step by step including photographs of the hands manipulating the rope, thus the reader should have no difficulty in following any sequence.

Four individual strands have been used, even for

knots which can and very often are made on the three strands of an unlaid rope. To avoid repetition such knots and/or plaits are indicated throughout with an asterisk. Others, such as the track knot, which would be made only on stranded rope, are shown accordingly.

In case the whole may appear awesome, two things may be said. Firstly, an understanding of Knots 2, 4 and 6 is all that is needed to complete the bell toggle (right) (Knot 48). Secondly, however complicated any piece may appear it is only a multiplicity of simple twists (turns) and bends (bights) locked into position. The star knot is an ideal example as it looks difficult, yet there are only six basic movements, repeated on each of as many strands as are employed.

As far as usage is concerned one does not have to be a seaman or yacht owner to appreciate the application of 'tiddly' ropework, even in the home. Try covering a queer-shaped bottle to make a standard lamp, for instance. Naturally it has more applications, certainly too numerous to specify, aboard even the smallest of boats. The onus must be left to the imagination of the owner.

To say the least, any metal handle provides a more secure and warmer grip if covered, particularly if it is a question of hanging on to it hour after hour in heavy weather, whilst hand grips on shrouds, rails etc can be very useful—so why not make them 'tiddly'?

1
To Wall Any Number of Strands

Pass each strand around under its neighbour, working anti-clockwise, Fig 1, and pass the last strand up through the bight of the first (held on the thumb), Fig 2. In a correct wall all strands emerge separately from the top, pointing upwards. Any number of strands may be used and it can be made backwards (ie clockwise).

Double Wall*
The emerging strands, Fig 3, lay alongside previous bights which are 'followed around' until all again emerge separately from the top, pointing upwards as in Fig 4. The knot has been shown 'flat' but when hauled tight it assumes a vertical form, the 'followed around' strands resting on the *wall* below.

Continuous Walling
Suitable only for covering any cylindrical object due to the hollow centre which develops. Strands are whipped to the object and walls made one on top of another, Fig 5A.

Wall Plait*
A reasonably tight plait can be made by continuous walling without a central heart provided not more than four strands are used, Fig 5B.

*Indicates throughout knots using four individual strands that can be made on three strands of an unlaid rope (see Introduction).

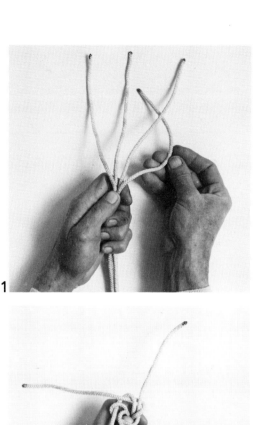

1

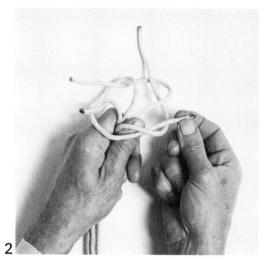

2

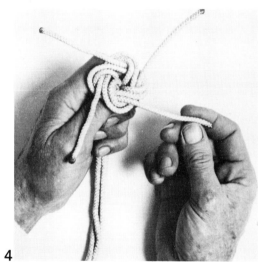

3

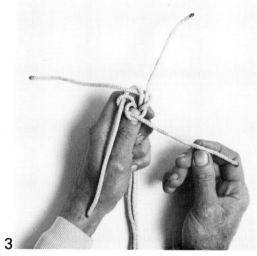

4

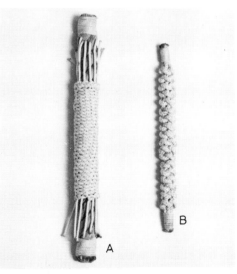

5

A

B

2
To Crown Any Number of Strands

Pass each strand around over its neighbour working anti-clockwise, Fig 1, and the last strand down through the bight of the first, Fig 2. All strands should emerge separately from the bottom, pointing downwards, Fig 3. It can also be made backwards (clockwise) and any number of strands used.

Double Crown*
Form the crown as shown in Fig 3, pull back any one strand and make a clockwise turn around the strand it has passed over, returning it to its original position, Fig 4. Repeat with the other three strands, the last passing through the double bight of the first, Fig 5.

Continuous Crowning
This is another method of covering any cylindrical object, by forming one crown on top of another, Fig 6A.

Crown Plait, Spiral*
This is made by continuous crowning, anti-clockwise, without a central heart, not more than four strands being used, when a spiral effect will result, Fig 6B.

Crown Plait, Straight*
A straight, chain-like pattern will result if the crowns are made alternately anti-clockwise and clockwise, Fig 6C.

Wall and Crown Plait*
This is made by forming alternate walls and crowns, using not more than four strands, Fig 6D.

Note
Four strands when crowned also produce a square knot.

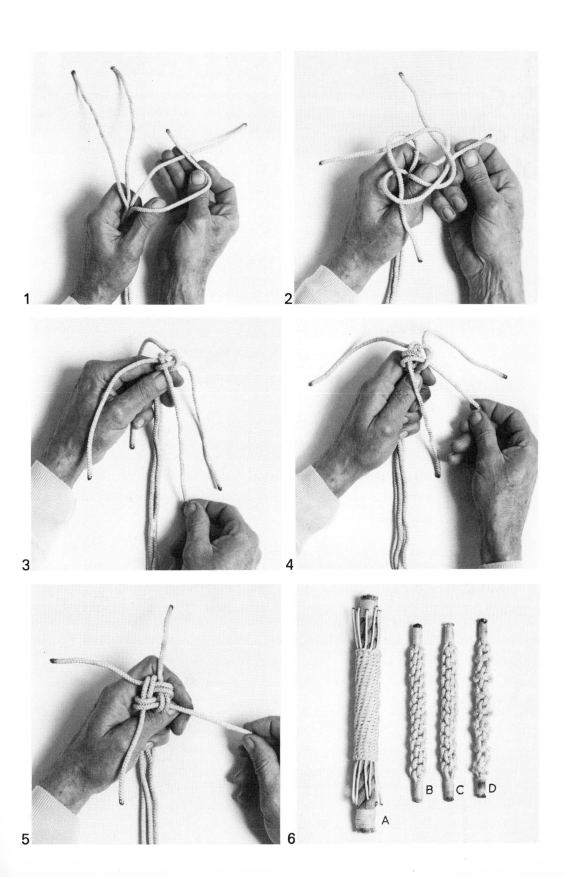

1

2

3

4

5

6
A B C D

3
Flat Carrick Bend

Commencement of Diamond Knot and basis of Carrick Mat

This can be used as a working knot, but decoratively used it is the start of the diamond knot (Knot 4) or, when both ends emerge from the same side, the basis of the carrick mat (Knot 35).

It is shown here with short ends but would be made on a much longer cordage when making a diamond knot with single strand 'eye' (Knot 4).

The 'eye', which can be seen emerging on the right, Fig 4, must be kept clear of the main turns.

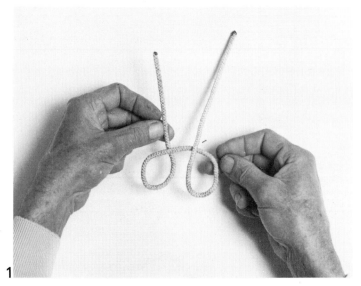

1

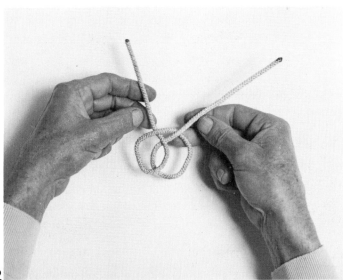

2

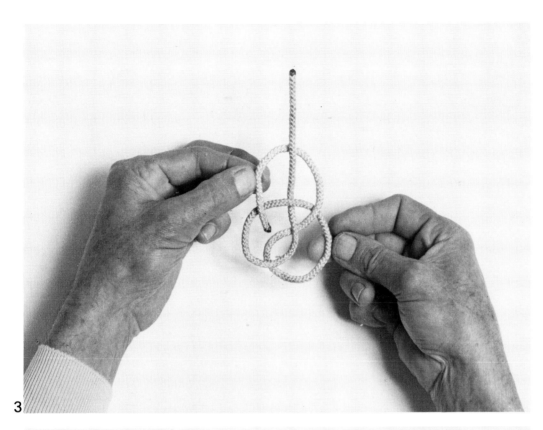

3

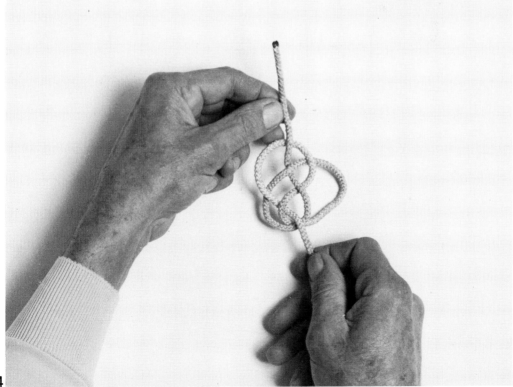

4

4
Diamond
Knot

*On the bight of one
strand*

A diamond knot can be incorporated into any scheme of decorative work, but in this form it would more likely be used as the commencement of a lanyard, bell toggle or other similar knots.

Having formed the flat carrick bend (Knot 3) it remains only to lead the two ends around the 'eye' in an anti-clockwise direction, haul both up through the centre of the original knot, Fig 5, and by working the turns towards the 'eye', Fig 6, arrange and haul tight, Fig 7.

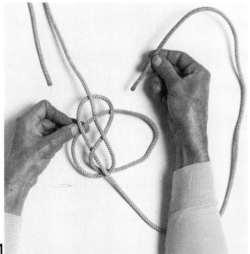

1

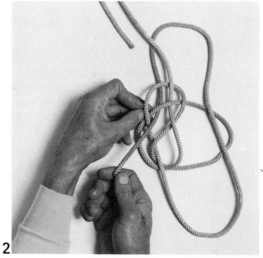

2

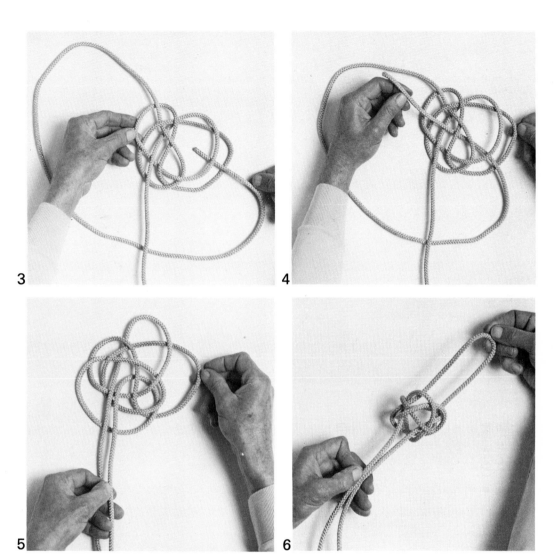

3

4

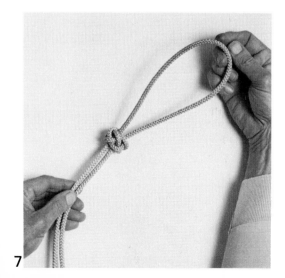

5

6

7

5
Diamond Knot, On Four Strands*

A bight is formed in all strands, Fig 1. Each strand is then taken anti-clockwise past the adjacent bight and up through the next, Figs 2 to 6.

Double Diamond Knot*

From the single diamond, each strand is 'followed around' until all again emerge from the top. Because the original knot was made by passing one bight before going up through the next, each 'follow around' strand passes under two parts, the last under two double parts, Fig 9B.

Diamond Hitching

Continuous diamond knotting can be used to cover any cylindrical object, and consists of one diamond knot on top of another, Fig 9A.

Diamond Plait

This can be made with one diamond knot on top of another but a tighter plait is obtained if crowns are made between the diamonds. Fig 9C shows single and double diamond knots with crowns between.

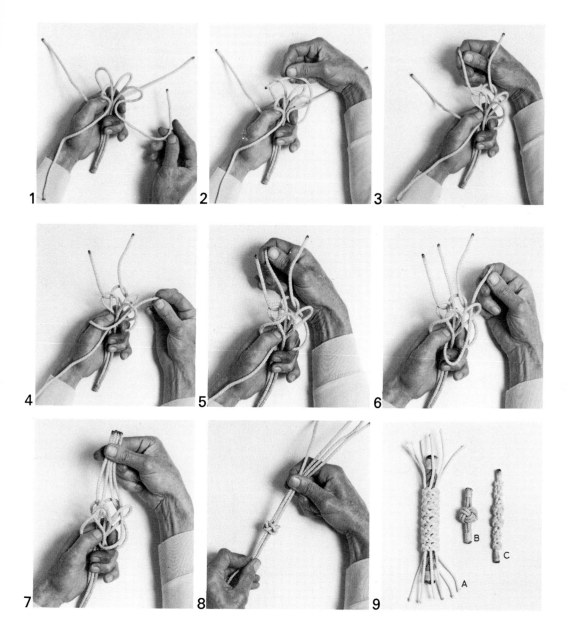

1

2

3

4

5

6

7

8

9

6
Star Knot,
Six
Stranded

All strands are looped *backwards*, Figs 1 and 2, and the tails brought up through the next loop working anti-clockwise, Figs 3 and 4. All are next crowned *backwards*, Figs 5 and 6. Reverting to anti-clockwise working, each strand is brought back around and up under its own part, Fig 7, forming six more loops above the originals, Fig 8. Each strand will be found to lay alongside a previous tuck, pointing directly to an appropriate pair of loops down through which all are tucked, Figs 9 and 10. The knot is turned upside-down, Fig 11, all strands again following a previous tuck, over two and down through the centre when they all emerge together, Fig 12.

The more strands used the better the result, six being shown to do the knot justice whilst ensuring photographic clarity. Any fewer will be unsatisfactory, especially four, which will result in a glorified, un-starlike square knot, ideal however if that is the requirement.

7
Pineapple Knot, Four Stranded

Form a crown (Knot 2), pass each strand over the adjacent bight, under its neighbour and down through the next bight, Figs 1 and 2. Turn the work upside-down and make a *backwards* crown, Fig 3, which, when tightened, leaves each strand laying alongside a previous tuck, Fig 4. 'Follow around', as in Figs 5 and 6, then return the work the right way up and continue to 'follow around', Fig 7, until all the ends emerge separately at the bottom, pointing downwards. Tuck all the strands up through the centre when they emerge together, Fig 8. If used as a terminal knot the ends can be cut short or combed into a tassel.

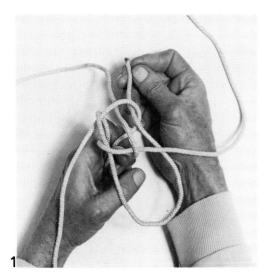

1

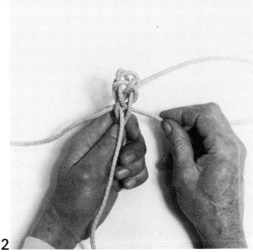

2

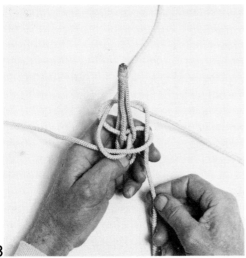

3

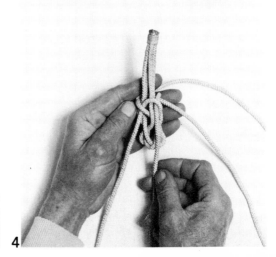

4

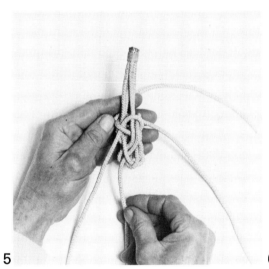

5

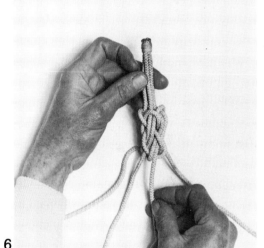

6

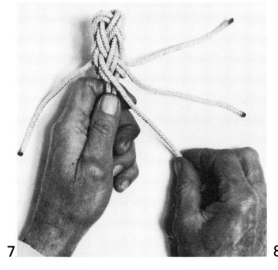

7

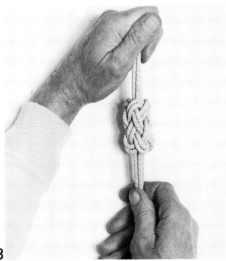

8

8
Rose Knot, Four Stranded*

Form a wall (Knot 1) and crown (Knot 2) as shown in Figs 1 and 2. Completely 'follow around' the wall, Fig 3, but only partially 'follow around' the crown, Fig 4. Pass all the strands down through the centre, Fig 5, to emerge separately as shown in Fig 6. Form a further wall, Fig 7, then a diamond knot (Knot 5), Fig 8, which is 'followed around', Fig 9, and all ends taken up through the centre and cut short, Fig 10.

Wall and Crown*
This is a knot in its own right, Fig 2, at which stage the ends would be cut short.

Manrope Knot*
If, after completing Fig 3, the crown was completely 'followed around' and the ends cut short, the result would be a manrope knot.

Stopper Knot*
This is made by forming the crown first, followed by a wall and both then being 'followed around' (not illustrated).

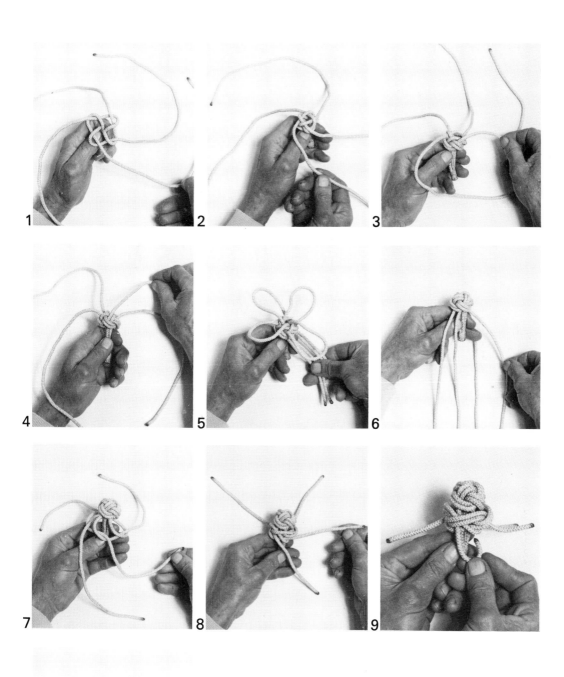

9
Tack Knot *

The tack knot is a real old-timer and though little used today is nonetheless a useful decorative knot. A modern sail still has its 'tack' even if it is no longer secured by a tack knot. It is invariably made on a rope's end and can easily be mistaken for a manrope or stopper knot.
As distinct from either, it is a double wall (Knot 1), double crowned (Knot 2), Fig 1 showing the double wall and Fig 2 the double crown on top. The ends are then tucked down through the knot, Fig 3, tapered as Fig 4, and finally served, Fig 5.

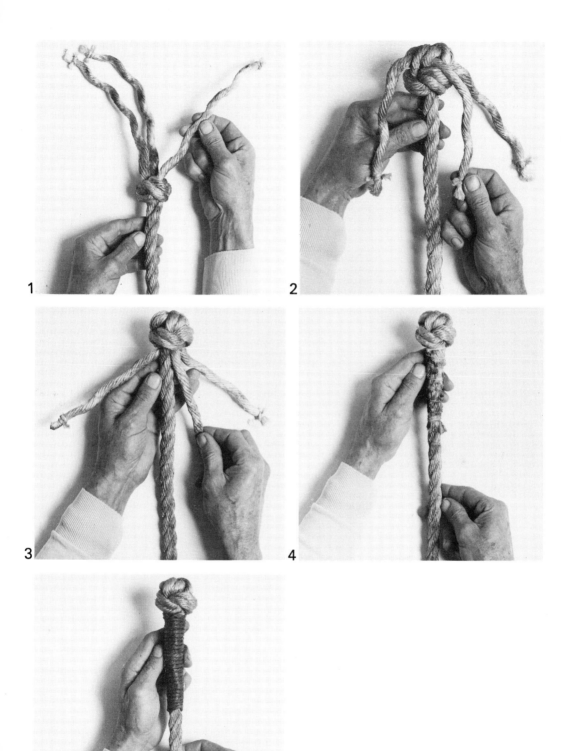

1

2

3

4

5

10 Single and Double Matthew Walker *

Single and double Matthew Walker knots are usually made on laid rope at some position throughout its length, the rope then being made up again as shown. However, they can be made on an end which is then whipped or even multi-stranded.

To make the single Matthew Walker any strand is taken around, under the other two and a bight retained, Fig 1. The second strand is taken around, passed up through this bight and a second bight retained, Fig 2. The third strand is next taken around, up through the first bight, Fig 3, and on, up through the second bight, Fig 4, the finished knot when worked tight appearing as in Fig 9A.

Double Matthew Walker *

In this case any strand is taken around, under the other two and brought up through its own bight, Fig 5. The second is brought around, up through this bight, Fig 6 and on up through its own bight, Fig. 7. The last strand is brought around, up through both these bights in turn and on up through its own bight, Fig 8, the finished knot when worked tight appearing as shown in Fig 9B.

Note
These knots would normally be made 'in the hands' but have been shown 'flat' to ensure maximum clarity.

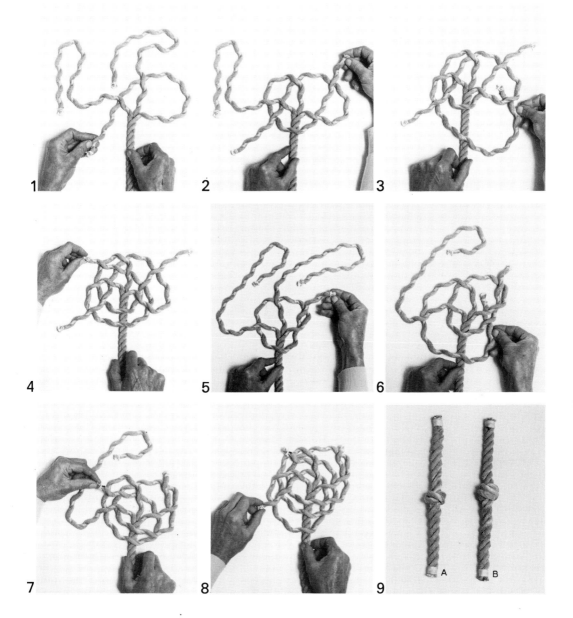

11 Decorative Shamrock Knot

This knot is made by working three bights and both ends, tucking each in turn under the previous one in a clockwise direction, Figs 1 to 4, with the completed first stage drawn tight, as shown in Fig 5.

The bights and ends are then crowned in the normal manner, Figs 5 and 6, whilst the finished knot, Fig 7, will be found to have the same appearance, front and back.

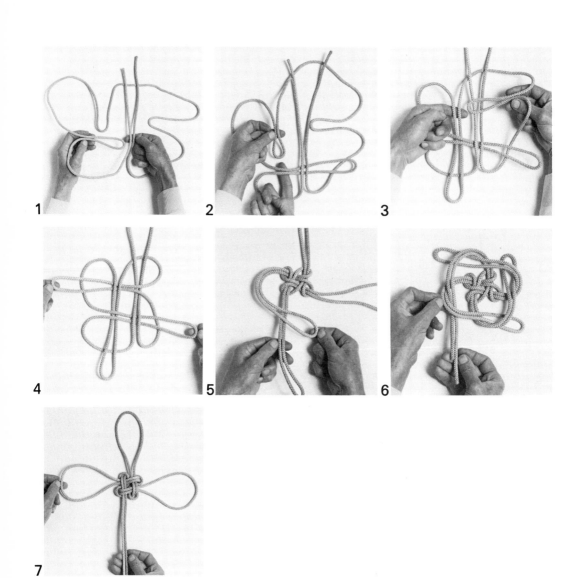

Apart from the fact that it is an intriguing knot as its name implies, the fool's knot, although it cannot be claimed to be decorative, is included since it provides the commencement of the square plait (Knot 16).
As a working knot it forms the basis for several others but as a trick knot, few people, having had it demonstrated to them, will succeed the first time in trying to make it.

12
Tom Fool's Knot
Commencement of Square Plait

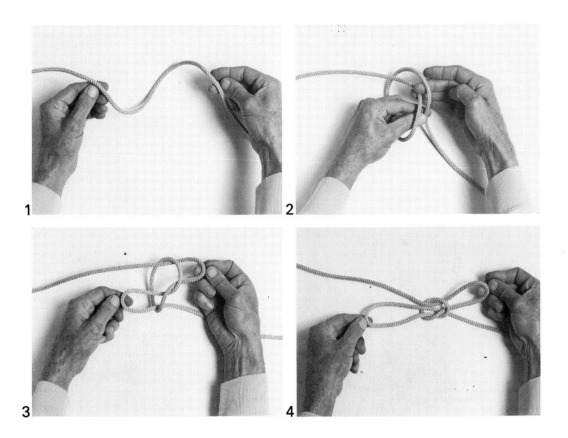

13
Turk's Head Knot

One of the most versatile decorative knots, usually applied to any cylindrical object, occasionally flattened into a turk's head mat or, as shown, tightened into a knot. The most simple version is illustrated (ie minimum *turns* and *parts*) made 'on the hand' to show the reverse side by rotation. The rope is set up as in Figs 1 and 2, then the hand rotated, Fig 3. The bights are then crossed, and the working end tucked right to left, Figs 4 and 5, then back, left to right as in Fig 6, at which point the working end meets the standing part in parallel for the first time, Fig 7. The work is 'followed around', Fig 8 showing the first and Fig 9 the second full circuit, the whole then being worked into a tight knot, Fig 10.

Turk's Head
This is complete in Fig 9, and may be transferred to any cylindrical object, being worked tight in the normal manner.

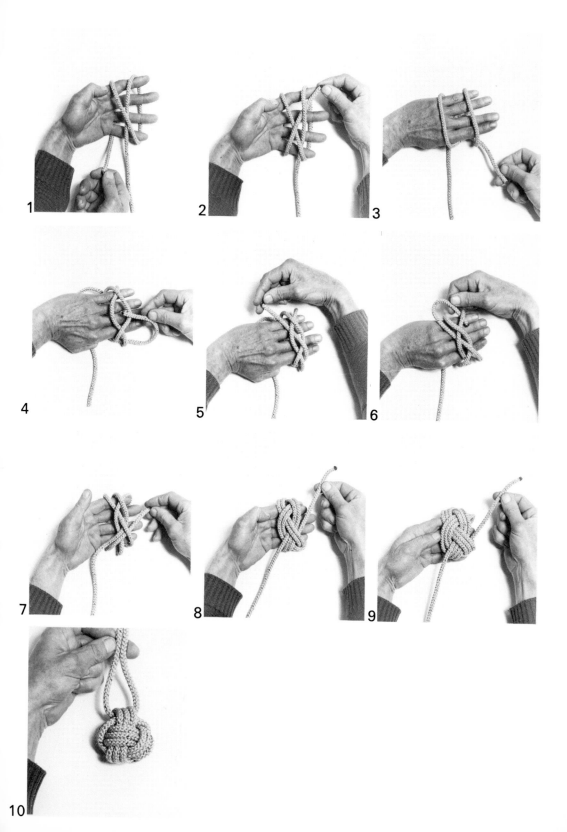

14
Chain Plait

Sometimes called a drummer's plait when it was used to decorate such instruments, it is commenced with an overhand (or thumb) knot except that one side is a bight, not an end, Figs 1 and 2.

Thereafter it is simply a question of raising bight through bight, Figs 3 and 4, for the required length of plait which is then finished off by reeving the end through the last bight as can be seen in the completed work, Fig 5.

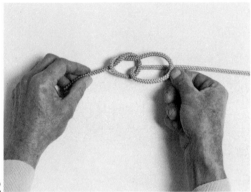

1

2

3

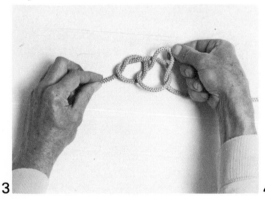

4

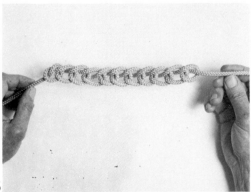

5

The figure of eight is a knot in its own right and this plait is simply a series of such knots all interwoven. Figs 1 and 2 show the initial figure of eight, Figs 3, 4 and 5, the second, after which the process is repeated until the plait is of the required length.

The amount of tension is a matter of choice, the completed work, Fig 6, having been left loose for clarity. It could be 'followed around' indefinitely if so desired, by passing the working end back and forth, when it could become an elongated section of a mat.

15
Double
Chain Plait

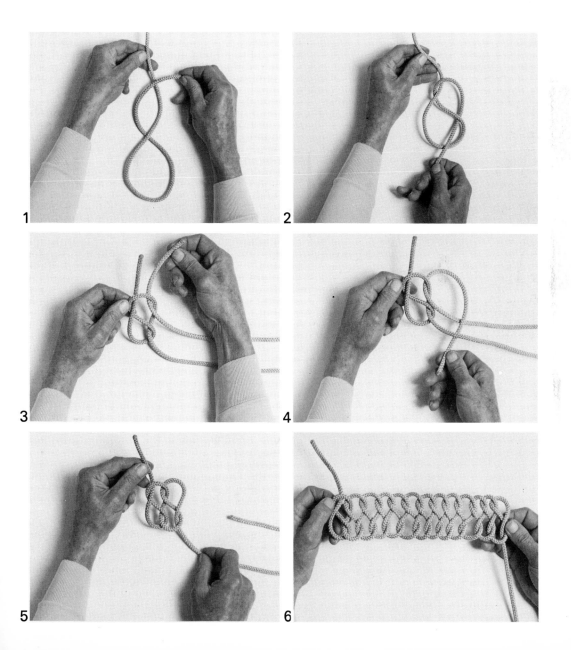

16
Square Plait

This plait has the appearance of square sennit with the advantage that it is made on a single strand much more quickly and easily.

A tom fool's knot (Knot 12) is made, Fig 1, after which a bight of the standing part is drawn through the right-hand loop, where it is gripped by pulling back on one strand of the left-hand loop, Fig 2.

The process is repeated with a bight through the left-hand loop, Fig 3, hauled tight by one strand of the right-hand loop and so on for the required length, working alternately from side to side, Fig 4.

To finish off the plait in such manner that it will not unravel, the end instead of the bight is passed through the last but one loop and back through the last, Fig 5, the finished plait appearing as in Fig 6.

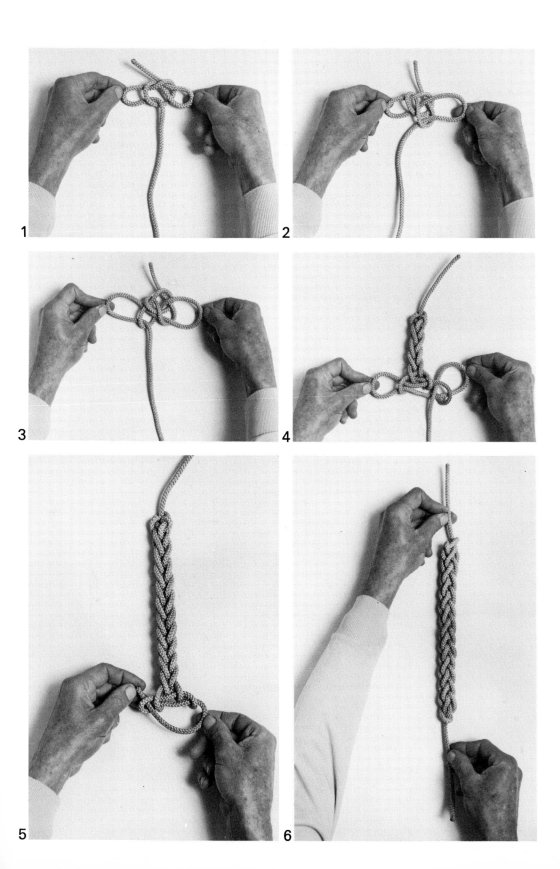

1

2

3

4

5

6

17
Twist Plait

The length of the plait is established by the size of the bight, Fig 1, which is then twisted in a clockwise direction, Fig 2, and the end passed through to the left, Fig 3. The bight is then twisted anti-clockwise, Fig 4 and the end passed through to the right, Fig 5, the whole process being repeated until the required length is completed, Fig 6.

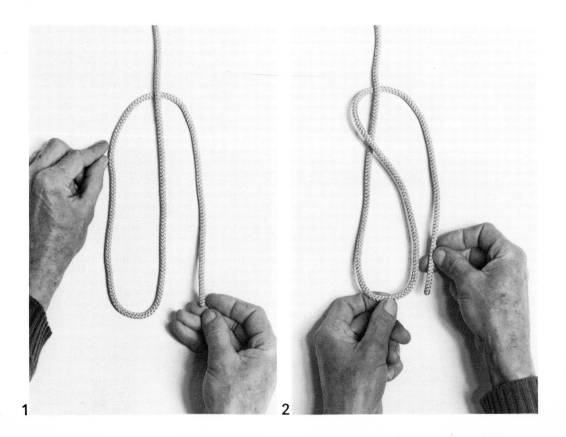

1   2

3

4

5

6

18 Overhead Knot Plait, Four Stranded

This plait can be made from four separate strands whipped together or, as shown on two strands, crossed at right-angles at their centres.

An overhand (thumb) knot is made on the lower strand trapping the upper strand, Fig 1. The upper strand is next knotted in the same way around the first knot, Fig 2, and so on, alternately to completion of the required length, Fig 3.

This is undoubtedly one of the most simple of plaits but to maintain a constant, symmetrical pattern every knot must be made in the same direction, ie, if the knots are started left over right all must be maintained so. A variation of pattern can be made by alternating the left over right/right over left sequence, but this must be regular and becomes a matter of practice and choice.

1

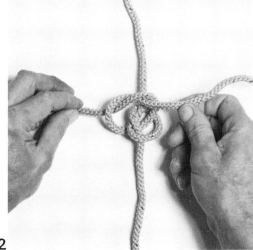

2

3

As with the four strand version this plait may be made on the ends of eight strands or, as shown, on the bights of four. Thereafter it becomes a doubled version of the four strand, using pairs of overhand knots, care being taken to keep them symmetrical.

19 Overhand Knot Plait, Eight Stranded

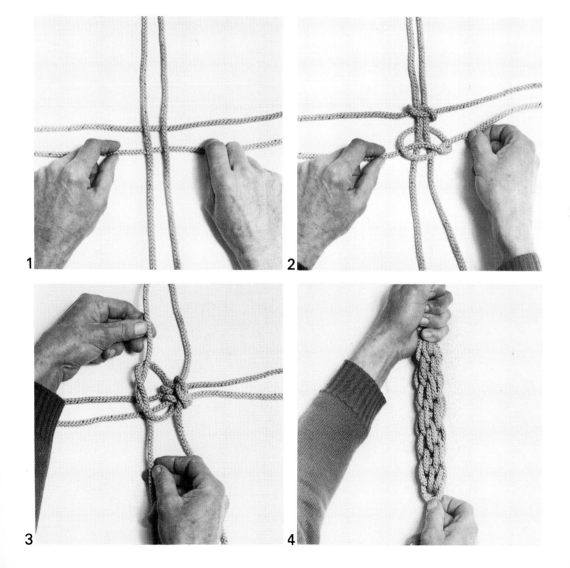

1

2

3

4

Sennits

Whether they be flat, round, square or spiral, common, English, French, Portuguese or Russian, sennits may be broadly divided into three groups: those that can be made with any number of strands; those that can only be made with any odd number; and those that require an even number. The square sennit is an exception, for although it requires an even number, it can be made only on eight, twelve or sixteen strands or a multiple, eight being the minimum.

A basic principle may be applied to the odd number group, in that the strands are divided with one more on one side than on the other, resulting in odd and even sides. Thereafter the outside strands each time, starting with the even side, are brought across to the centre and laid inside the previous odd number; thus the odd and even sides alternate as the work proceeds.

Note
As illustrated, a plastic binder such as is used to secure loose leaves of paper makes an ideal 'former' to secure any number of strands when making a sennit.

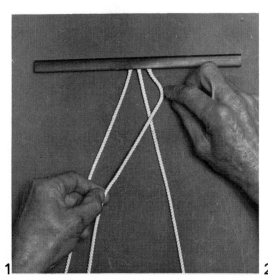

1

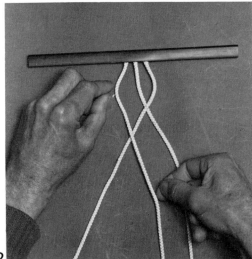

2

Obviously one of the odd number group, this is the most simple of all the sennit family, being most useful in mat-making when made up in long lengths. Strands are arranged, two to the right and one to the left, then the outside right is brought across to the inside of the left-hand strand, Fig 1. Outside left is next brought across to inside right, Fig 2, and the new outside right returned to become inside left, Fig 3.

All three strands have now been moved for the first time, Fig 4, showing them drawn tight, after which the process is continued to completion of any required length, Fig 5.

20 Common Sennit, Three Stranded

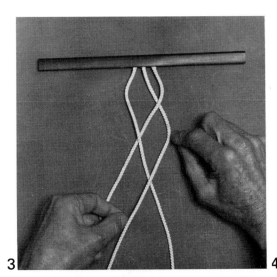

3

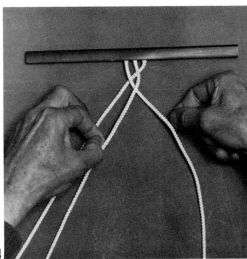

4

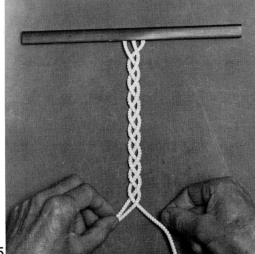

5

21
Common Sennit, Seven Stranded

Again one of the odd number group, it is a more elaborate version of the three strand, the same principles being applied. Figs 1 to 4 show the movements of the first four strands after which the 'lay' becomes automatic, all seven having been woven loosely in, Fig 5, and completed, Fig 6.

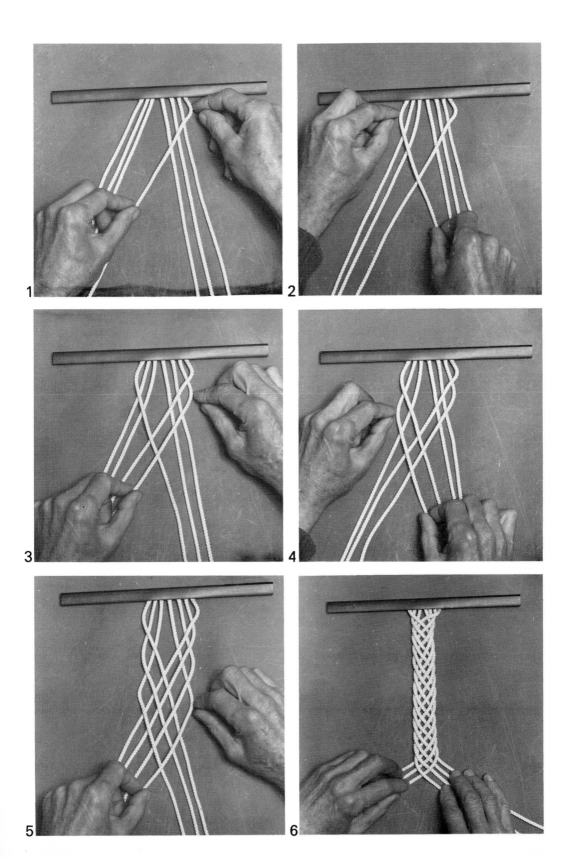

22
Round
Sennit, Six
Stranded

Four strands being the minimum, this sennit is made with any even number of strands and although it would normally be made vertically, it is shown 'flat' for maximum clarity.

It consists of taking alternate strands anti-clockwise around and over their immediate neighbours, the first strand, Fig 1, and all three strands, Fig 2, after which each is drawn down, Figs 3 and 4, leaving three strands 'up'. The 'up' strands are next taken clockwise over each of the 'held down' strands (which are released in passing), Fig 5, showing the first and all three in Fig 6, before the clockwise strands are in turn 'held down', Figs 7 and 8. The first three are again taken anti-clockwise and the whole process continued, when the sennit begins to take shape, Fig 9, a completed length appearing as in Fig 10.

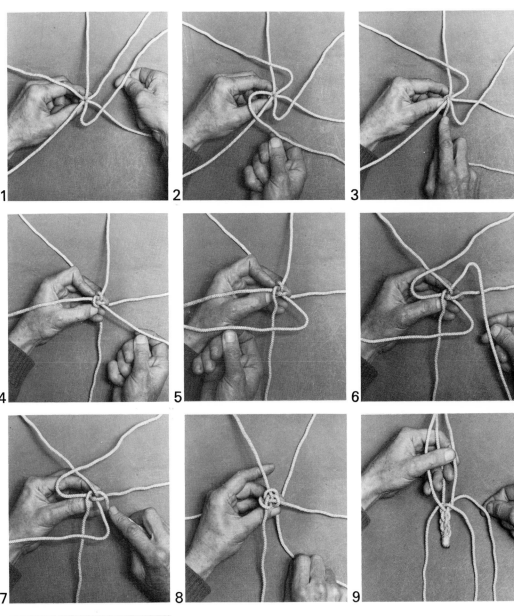

23
Square
Sennit, Eight
Stranded

This must be made, not only with an even number of strands but with multiples, either eight, twelve or sixteen, the minimum being shown to illustrate the basic principle. The strands are separated equally, as in Fig 1, the outside right-hand strand brought under its fellows and on, up through the centre of the left-hand four, Fig 2, drawn tight, Fig 3, before being returned to its own side, where it is laid on the inside of the existing three, Fig 4. The outside left-hand strand is treated in the same way, emerging in the centre of the four right-hand strands, Figs 5 and 6, before being returned to its own side, Fig 7. Working alternate outside strands the sennit is continued, Fig 8, drawn tight in Fig 9, and to completion of any required length, Fig 10.

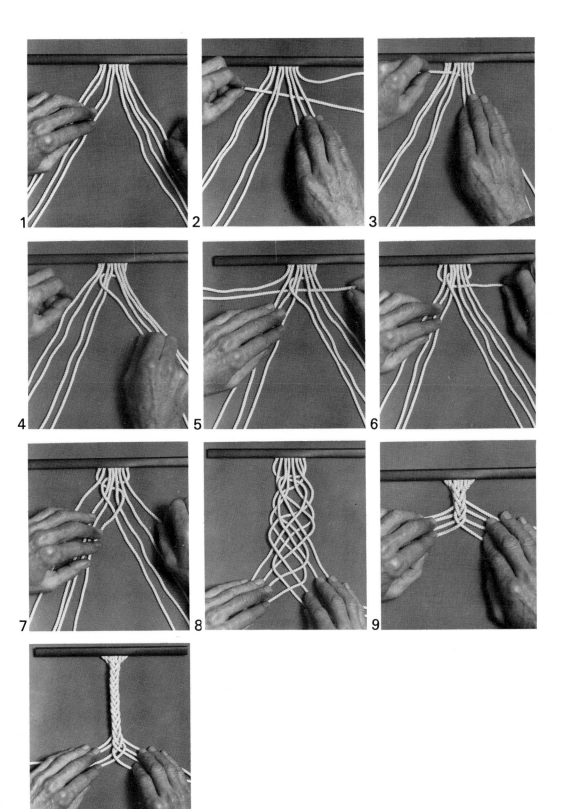

24 English Sennit, Seven Stranded

Seven strands have been used for no particular reason as this sennit can be made with any number, odd or even, with a minimum of four (three reverts to being a common sennit).

Each outside right strand is used in turn, being reeved under one/over one until it emerges on the opposite side where it is laid parallel and becomes the extreme left-hand strand. Figs 1 and 2 show the first and second strands so treated, all seven strands having been reeved for the first time in Fig 3, whilst Fig 4 shows a completed length, suitably tightened.

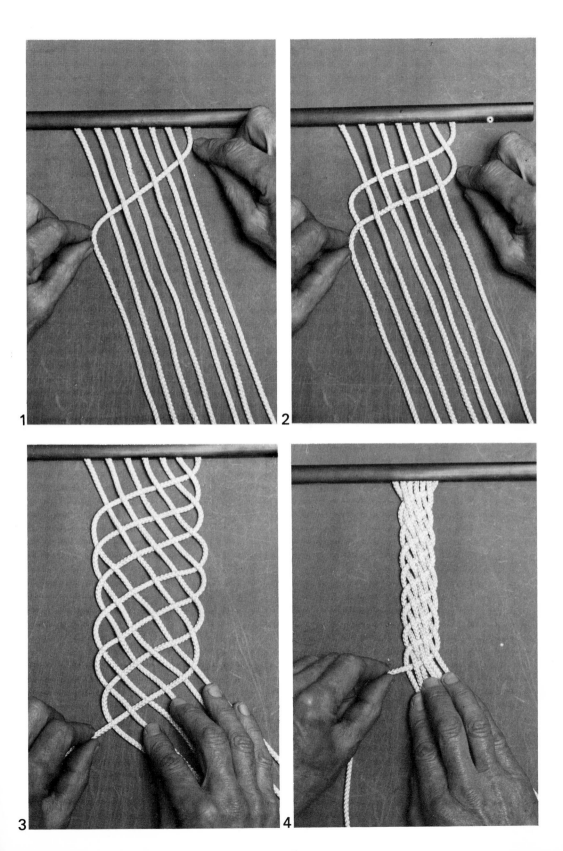

25
French
Sennit,
Seven
Stranded

As with the English sennit (Knot 24) the strands of the French are reeved under one/over one, but an odd number is necessary (five being the minimum) and they do not pass across the full width of the sennit, but arrive from alternate sides at the centre, to become left- or right-handed respectively.

Strands are laid out, three to left, four to right, Figs 1 and 2 showing the first strand (the outside of the right-hand group) reeved through to the centre and laid with the left-hand group. Figs 3 and 4 show the second strand (the outside of the left-hand group) similarly treated and laid with the right-hand group.

Strands three, four and five follow, figs 5 to 7, and this process is continued for the required length, Fig 8 showing the loosely woven strands, worked tight in Fig 9.

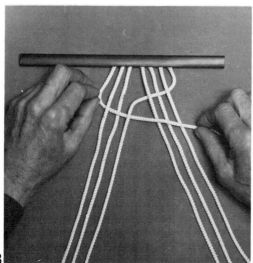

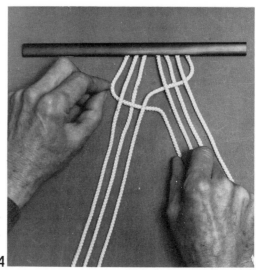

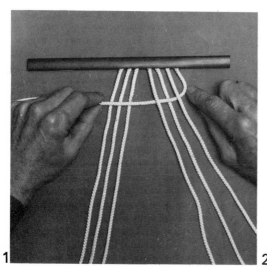

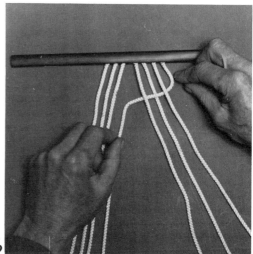

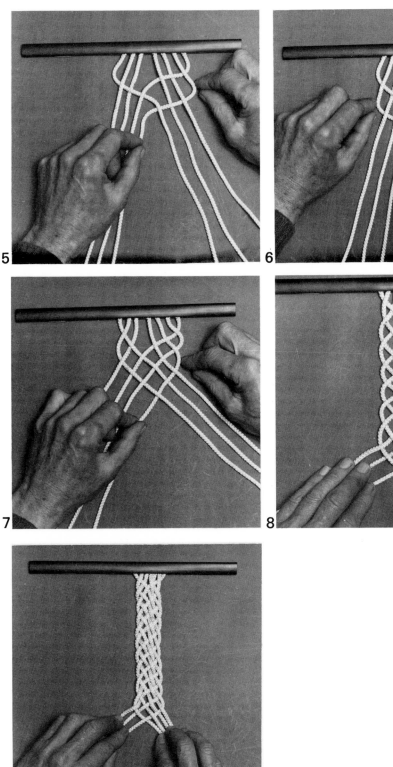

26 Portuguese Sennit, Spiral

There are only two working strands in a Portuguese sennit (these may be doubled if desired), one either side of a central heart, which can be any number of strands, usually two (more than three not being recommended).

The left-hand strand is passed under the hearts and over the right-hand strand, a bight being retained on the left, Fig 1. The right-hand strand is brought across, over the hearts, down through the bight, Fig 2, and both ends drawn tight, Fig 3. The left-hand strand is again passed under the hearts, Fig 4, the second knot being completed, Figs 5 to 7.

This process is continued, always using the left-hand strand first when the spiral will develop automatically, Fig 8, indeed it cannot be prevented or straightened out.

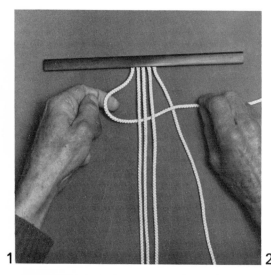

1

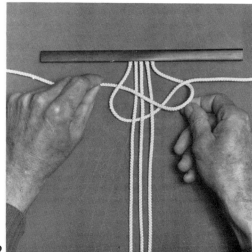

2

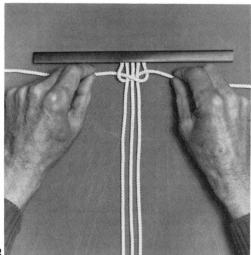

3

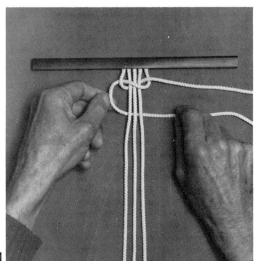

4

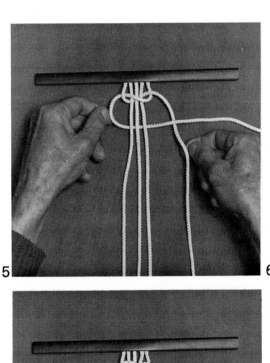

5

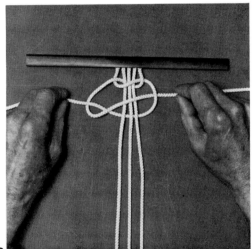

6

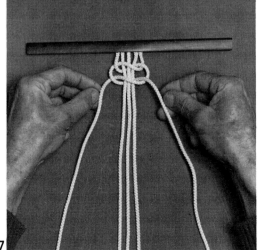

7

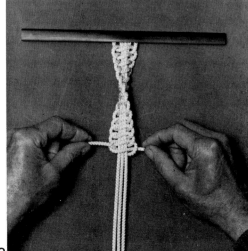

8

27
Portuguese Sennit, Flat

The arrangement of strands and formation of the first knot, Figs 1 to 3, are identical to the spiral version (Knot 26). The variation occurs at this point with the right-hand end being passed under the hearts, over the left-hand part, Fig 4, and the second knot completed as shown in Figs 5 and 6. The third knot is made in the same way as the first and so on with alternate left- and right-hand knots to completion, Fig 7.

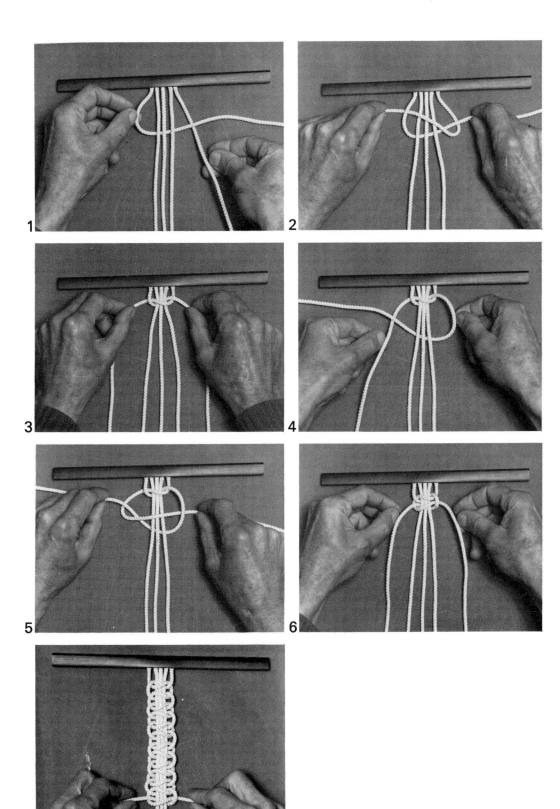

28 Spanish Hitching, Overhand and Reversed

There are two types of Spanish hitching, both being a means of covering any cylindrical object but, as distinct from continuous crowning (Knot 2), they involve the use of a 'warping strand' which is wound around and around the cylinder, interweaving the working strands, with every turn.

The latter are secured around the object in such numbers that they either completely fill the circumference or, as illustrated, with gaps between them. The thinnest possible warp would be used with the former, becoming almost indiscernible, whilst the heavier warp of the latter becomes an integral part of the pattern.

Fig 1 shows the working strands secured with a whipping and the 'warping strand' attached. The working strands must be kept *outside* the warp throughout. Pass the first working strand over the warp and back down, Fig 2, pulling both strand and warp tight. Rotate the work and repeat with the second strand and so on. Fig 3 shows the first full turn, Fig 4 the second, to completion in Fig 5.

Spanish Hitching, Reversed

A completely different pattern is obtained by keeping the working strands *inside* the warp and taking a full backwards round turn each time.

Fig 6 shows the warp and first working strand, with the turn taken in Fig 7.

This is repeated with each strand in turn, the first full rotation of the work being shown in Fig 8, the second in Fig 9, and the completed job, Fig 10.

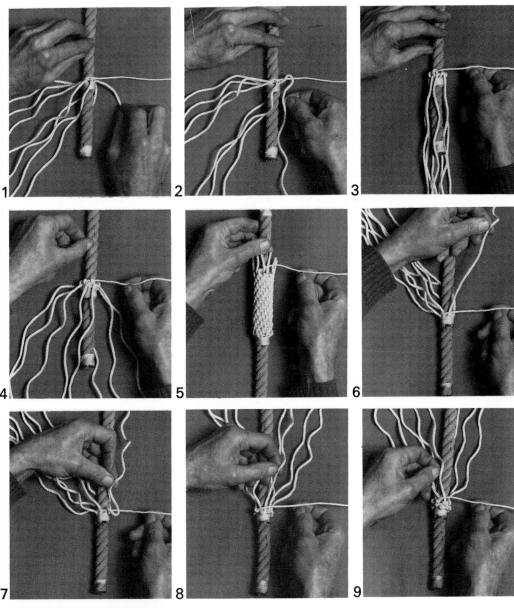

1

2

3

4

5

6

7

8

9

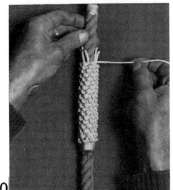

10

29 Russian Sennit, Six Stranded

The first and last strands form the border at each side around which the working strands are turned, four being shown, though any number may be used.

The first working strand is turned around the left-hand border and under the second working strand, Fig 1, before being laid away to the left, Fig 2. Each strand in turn, working left to right is tucked under its neighbour, also laid away to the left, Figs 3 to 5, and drawn tight with the last under the right-hand border, ready for the return, Fig 6.

All working strands are returned vertical and the border strand turned, Fig 7, after which the return reeving is made from right to left, Figs 8 to 10, thus completing the first 'over and back'. The completed length, Fig 11, is finished off by joining the border strands across the bottom and hitching the working strands to it (not illustrated).

Russian Mat

A square or rectangular mat can also be made on the same principle, using a large number of strands, obviously far too complicated to be photographed, even if necessary.

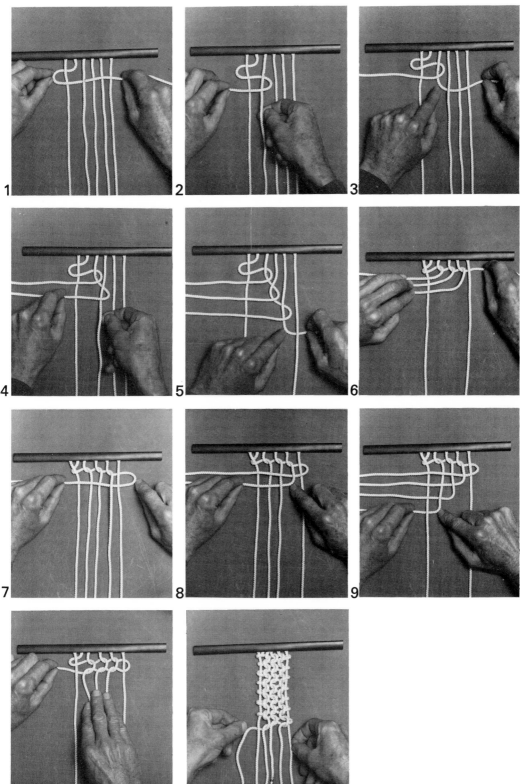

30
Cockscom-bing, Single Stranded

This is an ideal method of covering an object which is both cylindrical and circular as the gaps which form at the bottom of the bights are naturally taken up by the roundness of the ring.

It is essentially a question of making forwards and backwards hitches alternately, Figs 1 and 2, showing the formation of the first, drawn tight in Fig 3. The next hitch is made backwards, Figs 4 and 5, and so on alternately, Figs 6 and 7, until the ring is completely covered, Fig 8.

Cow Hitch
This is a useful knot provided that both standing parts share the load but usually it is the result of a wrongly made clove hitch, when it becomes useless. Fig 3 shows a typical cow hitch.

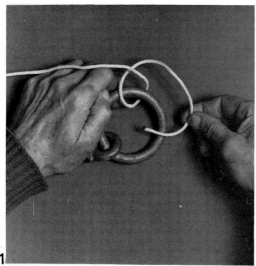

1

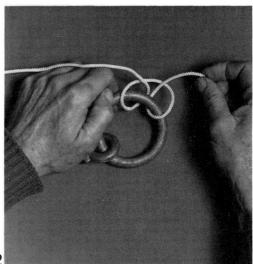

2

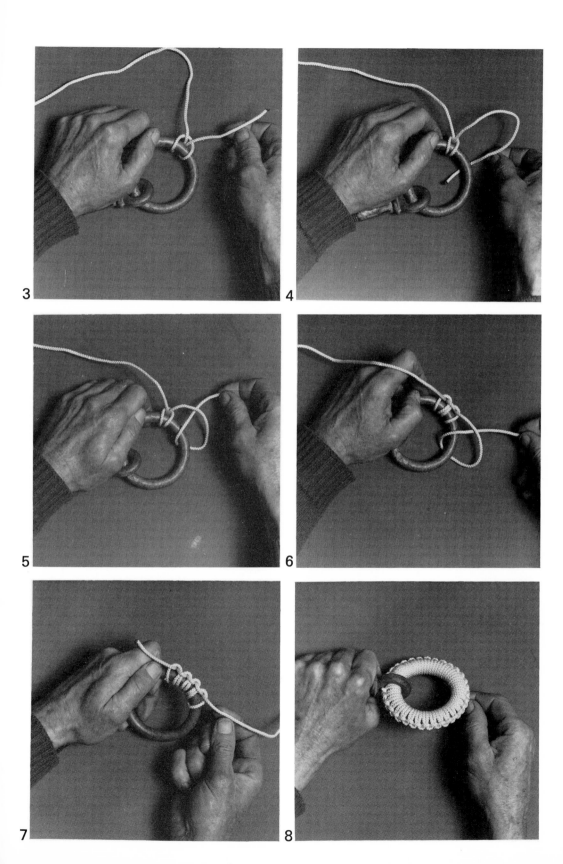

3

4

5

6

7

8

31 Cockscombing, Three Stranded

As illustrated three strands are normally used in this method of covering a cylindrical object, with the 'comb' being the feature. The three working strands are whipped to the object and a hitch made with the right-hand strand, Fig 1, drawn tight as in Fig 2.

The centre strand is then hitched in the same way but in the opposite direction and drawn tight, Figs 3 and 4, followed by the remaining left-hand strand, hitched in the same direction as the first, Fig 5. The process is then repeated, working each strand alternately right and left to completion, Fig 6.

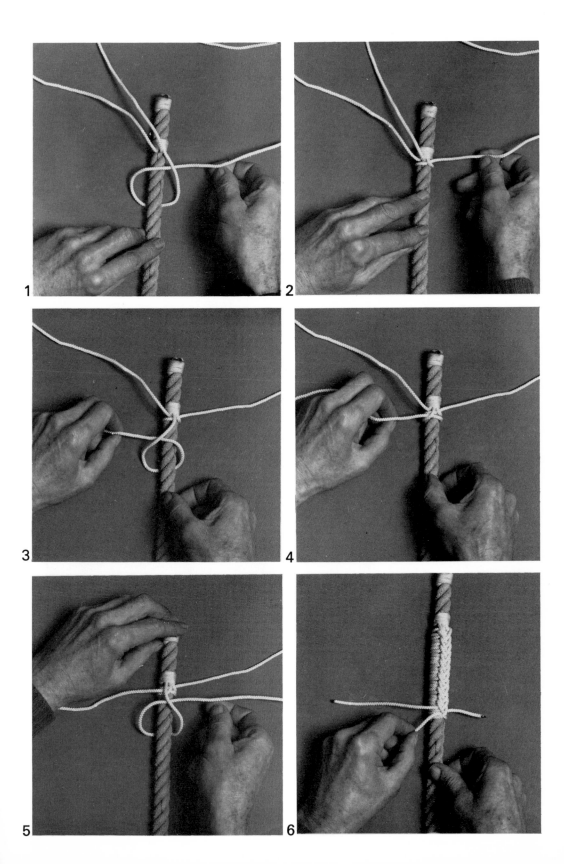

32
Thrum
Sennit

A thrum is a short piece of cordage, usually rope yarn (four to six inches long), but no rules prevent the use of plaited cordage, as illustrated.

Two thrums are laid down, Fig 1, a third added, Fig 2, the left-hand end of which is brought around, trapping two bights, before being laid parallel with the three right-hand strands, Fig 3, the top one of which is brought down to the vertical, Fig 4, resulting in one pair and one odd strand pointing downwards.

A fourth thrum is added, reeved through the bights of the first two (to prevent the whole from unravelling), Figs 5 and 6, brought to the parallel, Fig 7, and the top strand brought to the vertical, Fig 8. This completes the start and end sealing of the sennit with two pairs and one odd vertical strand.

The fifth thrum is laid down with the left-hand end emerging between the last pair and the odd strand, Fig 9, drawn tight, Fig 10, passed to the parallel, Fig 11, and the next top strand brought down, Fig 12. All further thrums are added in the same way as in Figs 9 to 12. On completion of the required length, the ends are trimmed to a given length, Fig 13, and can be left as such or combed into a fringe, Fig 14.

A long length of this sennit wound into a circle or formed into a square and sewn together makes the conventional door-mat with the bristle appearance. In the past, with slight variations, it was used also as anti-chafing gear, when it was made around topping lifts for instance, to protect the sails and was known as a 'Bag o' Wrinkles'.

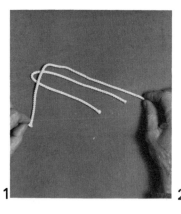

1

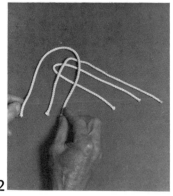

2

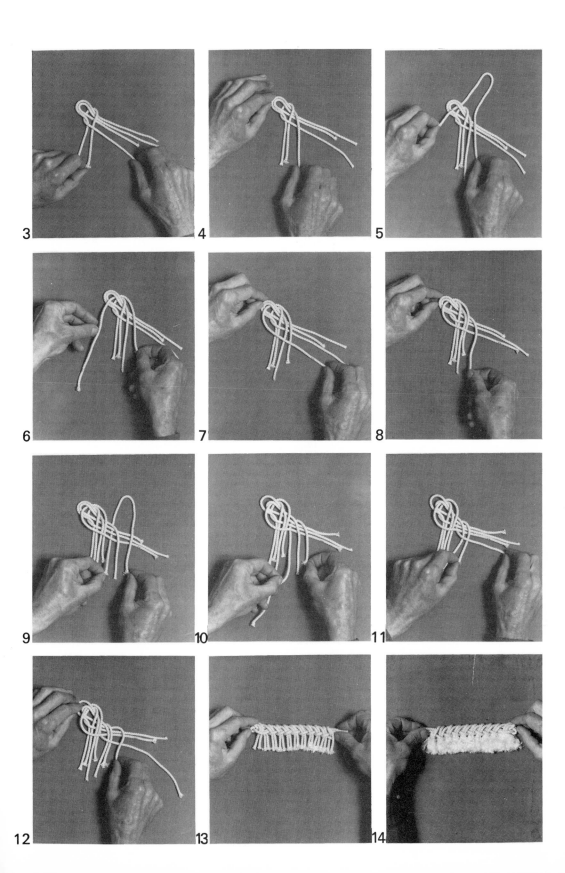

Mats

Although the name 'mats' is given to the following ropeworks, all except one are individually too small to be used as actual mats. The exception is the square mat, which is not 'followed around' and is the only one to increase equally in length and breadth with each additional bight being worked into it. However, there would be little beauty in one large square mat.

The art of mat-making is therefore the combination of a series of small mats conjoined with chosen sennits, all sewn together with sail twine. Those illustrated have been made with manufactured cordage purely for photographic clarity and whilst there are no rules against this, the beauty of any mat will be enhanced if the small mats are themselves made with sennit, the three stranded common sennit (Knot 20) being the most simple for this purpose. Knot 49 shows a suggested multiple mat, in this case made in miniature.

There are several other mats which border on weaving, the sword mat for instance requiring some sort of loom, whilst the wrought mat with its multiplicity of strands needs two pairs of hands. The Russian mat also requires a large number of strands which could become complicated, so a Russian sennit (Knot 29) has been illustrated, the mat being based on the same principle requiring only the additional strands to make up any given width.

A left-handed bight is laid down, followed by a right-hand bight laid on top, all arranged as in Fig 1, the standing part of this bight, Fig 1, bottom left, not again being used (unless the other end is found to be too short to complete the mat, when it may be used to 'follow around'). The upper left part is brought over this lower, laid under the bight, shown in Fig 2, and the end reeved over/under/over/under until it emerges at the top left-hand corner, Fig 3, when it is returned in a similar manner to the right-hand bottom corner, Fig 4. One further move, Fig 5, brings the working part back to the start of the mat. It remains only to 'follow around' for the first time, Fig 6, and the second, Fig 7, to complete the mat.

Tightness of the finished mat is a matter of choice, the one illustrated being left loose for clarity. Whilst the mat may be closed up completely, small gaps in the weave are useful in a working mat to allow for drainage.

33
Ocean Mat, Oval

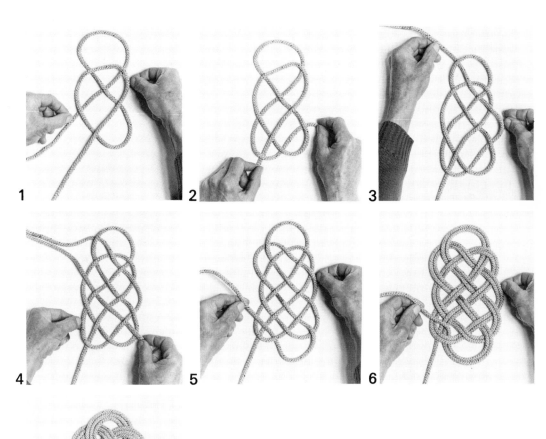

1   2   3

4   5   6

7

34
Ocean Mat, Square

This is one mat which is not 'followed around' and therefore can be made to any predetermined size. Two turned bights are laid down, Fig 1 (the longest and uppermost determining the diagonal size of the mat), the second bight having been dipped under the standing part of the first.

The top part only of this second bight, maintained in an elongated shape is dipped over/under and interlaced with the first bight, Fig 2, once again leaving two standing parts. The next move holds good for all further movements prior to the reeving of the bights.

The left-hand standing part is taken under the right-hand standing part and twisted anti-clockwise, Fig 3, before being reeved up through the mat, Figs 4 and 5, and finally elongated top and bottom, Fig 6. This is continued, the elongations becoming progressively shorter as the mat is infilled from diagonally opposite corners towards the middle (the opposite diagonal), Figs 7, 8 and 9.

Finally, the one end is taken under the remaining standing part, Fig 10, and reeved up to the opposite corner, completing the final diagonal and the finished mat, Fig 11.

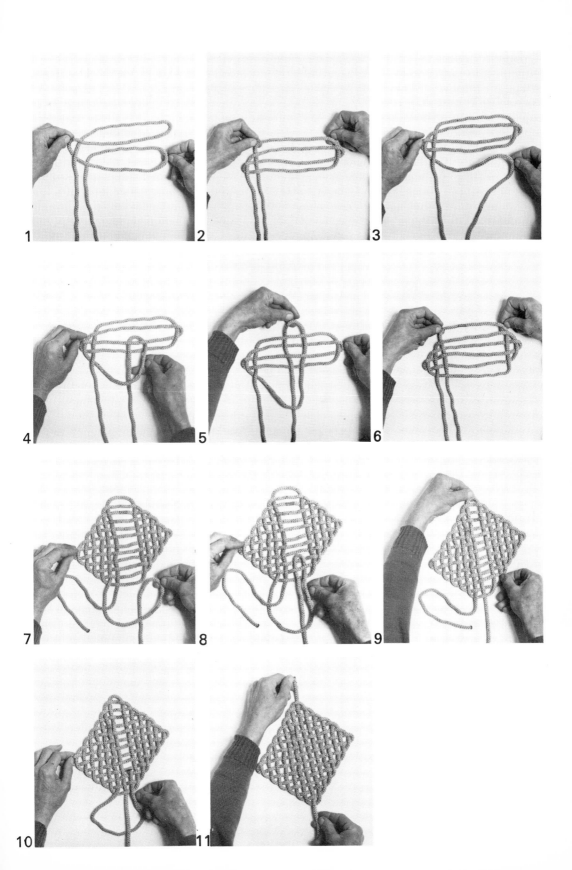

35
Carrick Mat

Two bights are laid up as in Fig 1, the left-hand part henceforth remaining static. The right-hand end is brought around, over this part to the top left-hand corner, Fig 2, and reeved through as shown in Fig 3.
Fig 4 returns the end to the start of the mat after which the first 'follow around' is made, Fig 5, and the completed mat, after the second 'follow around', Fig 6.

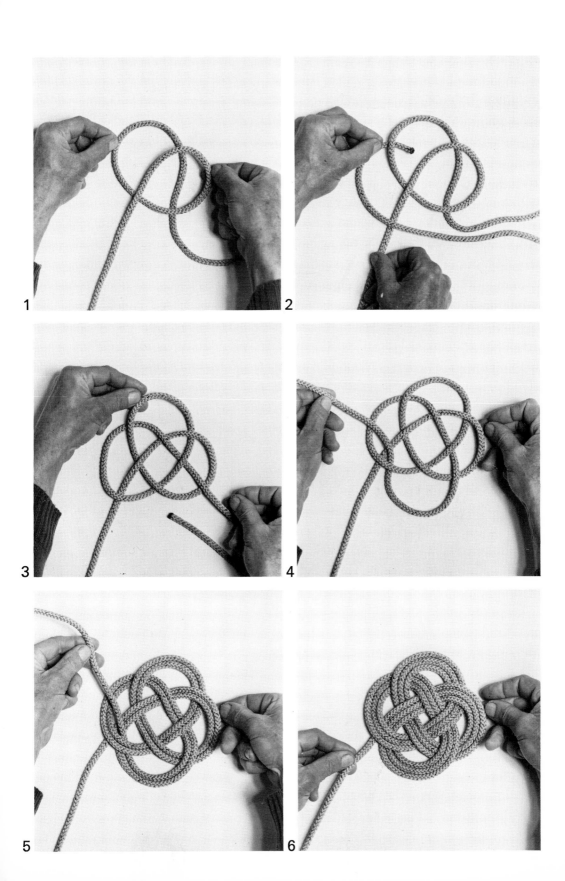

1

2

3

4

5

6

36
Jury Mat

This mat is based on a jury masthead knot, the bights of which are arranged as Figs 1 and 2, after which the centre bights are drawn out, over one/under one, to the extremities, Figs 3 to 6.

The new central bights, Fig 6, are crossed, the right-hand bight being on top of the left, the working end reeved through the centre of the mat from right to left, Fig 7, and returned to the start, Fig 8. It remains only to 'follow around' twice to complete the mat, Figs 9 to 12.

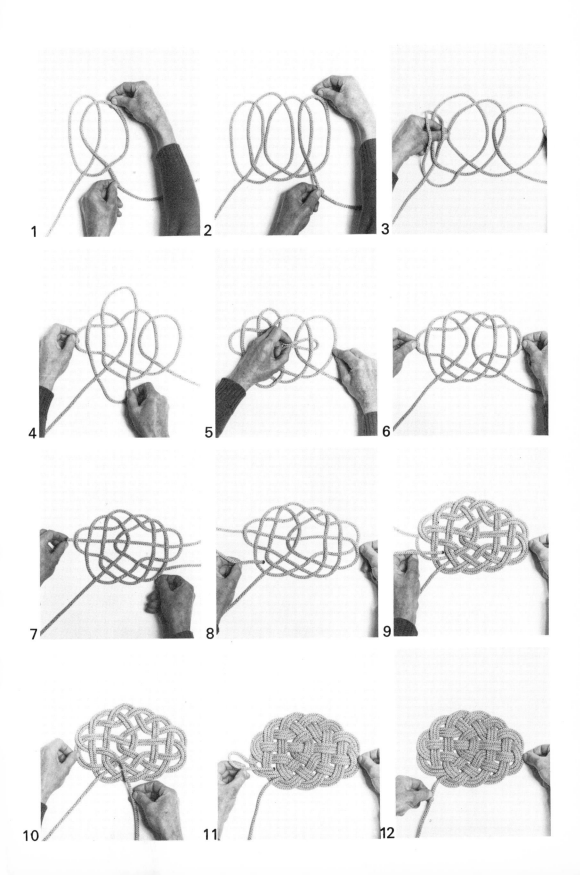

37
To 'Point' a Rope's End

The purpose of pointing a rope, apart from decoration, is to provide a stiff, tapered end to ensure speed and ease when reeving it through a block.

A whipping is applied, the rope unstranded, perimeter strands set aside, with the remainder tapered and bound. The method shown involves a warp (similar to Spanish hitching) which is attached, all as illustrated in Fig 1. In the 'lay' illustrated, strands are worked in pairs, Fig 2, showing their positions ready for commencement. A turn is taken with the warp, all 'up' strands brought down and 'down' strands taken up, prior to a further turn of the warp, Fig 3 showing several turns. This procedure is repeated (dropping odd strands as the taper narrows) until the point is covered, when the ends are either secured with a whipping or half-hitched around the warp, the whole being finished with a Turks' head (Knot 13), Fig 4.

The most elementary lay is one strand up/one down, but various patterns can be obtained. Three down/one up, raising the 'down' strands one at a time, produces a spiral pattern for instance. Alternatively, both types of Spanish hitching can be used or the warp dispensed with and the point covered with continuous crowning (Knot 2) or similar.

To prevent the ends of long, working strands from becoming tangled they are best bundled and secured with a clove hitch, thus allowing only sufficient working length to be drawn out as required.

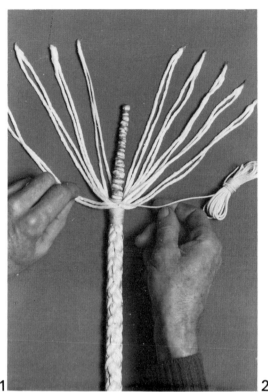

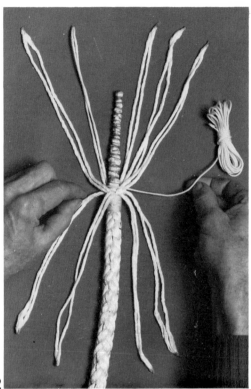

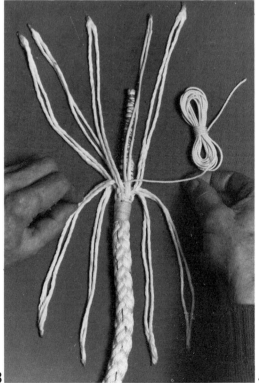

1

2

3

4

38
To Form a
Spindle Eye

A 'former', slightly larger in diameter than the required 'eye' is necessary, along which a number of ties (short lengths of cord) are laid and temporarily secured at both ends. The rope is prepared by applying a whipping, unlaying all strands, halving them and offering the whole up to the 'former', all as in Fig 1.

Each pair of strands is half-hitched over the 'former', care being taken to spread the hitches around the circumference to avoid bunching, Figs 2 and 3. The ends are returned to the standing part where they are tightly whipped, when the ties are released and knotted around the hitched strands, Fig 4.

The ends are tapered and tightly bound and the 'former' removed, Figs 5 and 6, when both 'eye' and taper are served, Fig 7. The finish is a matter of choice, Fig 8, showing the 'eye' covered with single strand Cockscombing with a Turk's head top and bottom of the taper.

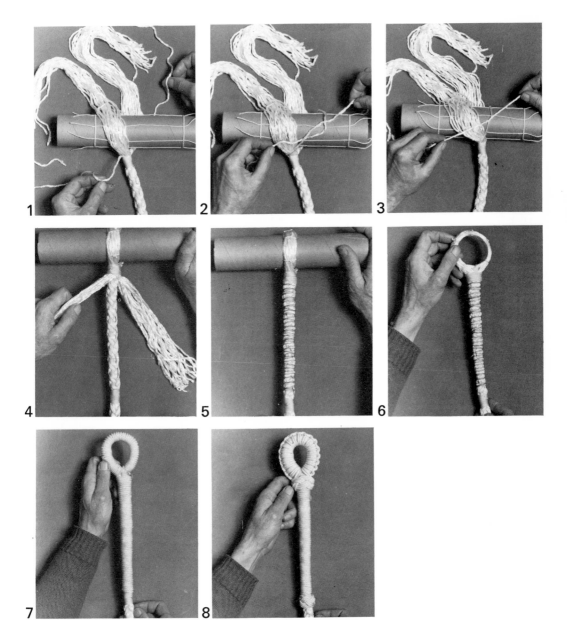

1 2 3
4 5 6
7 8

39
A Question of Bowlines: Left-Handed Bowline, Right-Handed Bowline

The bowline invariably found in everyday use could be called a left-handed bowline which is made with the same initial movements as the French bowline (Knot 40) and completed as illustrated in Fig 6A (ie omitting the second bight). There is a further type however, the prerogative of the old-time sailormen, the right-handed bowline, Fig 6B, the difference being that the tail lays clear of the bight. This can also be made in the usual manner with the obvious last move variation, but as a matter of interest it is shown made from two half-hitches when it becomes almost as great a challenge as the tom fool's knot (Knot 12).

The hitches are made on the standing part, Fig 1, the tail brought down and gripped over the lower part of the first hitch, Fig 2, then the standing part is hauled tight, Figs 3 and 4. The tail is turned outwards and the completed right-handed bowline appears as shown in Fig 5 (or Fig 6B).

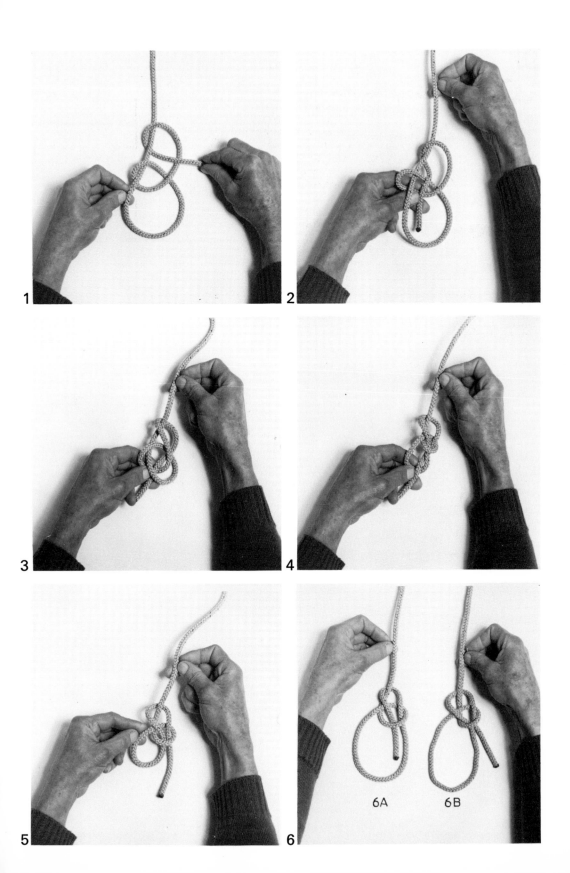

1

2

3

4

5

6

6A   6B

40
French
Bowline

The initial moves in making a French bowline are exactly the same as for the left- or right-handed bowlines (Knot 39), the tail being laid across the standing part, Fig 1, which is lifted over to form the bight with the end automatically 'up through', Figs 2 and 3.

In the French bowline the end is taken in a complete full turn, Fig 4, before being returned up through the loop, Fig 5, around the *standing part* and back down through both loop and bight, Fig 6.

This knot, producing two bights on a single end, is particularly useful where chafing of the bight is likely or when working with wire.

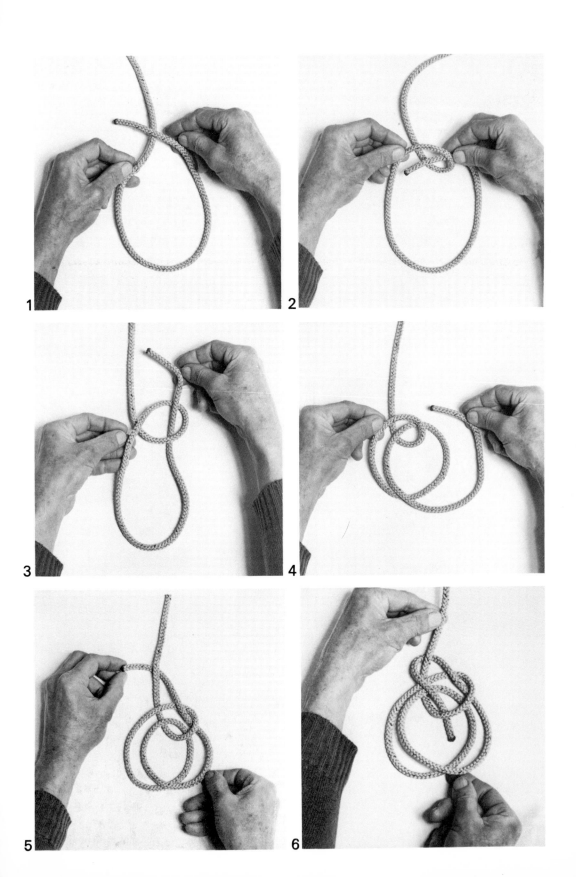

41
Spanish
Bowline

This knot is made on a bight and used under conditions where both standing parts are under load. It would normally be made 'in the hands' but is shown 'flat' to simplify the layout which consists of a series of bights, Fig 1, which becomes Fig 2 by crossing the large bight clockwise. The resulting top bight, Fig 2, is taken down, over the two small bights, Figs 3 and 4, and back up behind the standing part, Fig 5. Each side of this bight is tucked down through its respective small bights below, as shown in Fig 6, then hauled tight, Fig 7.

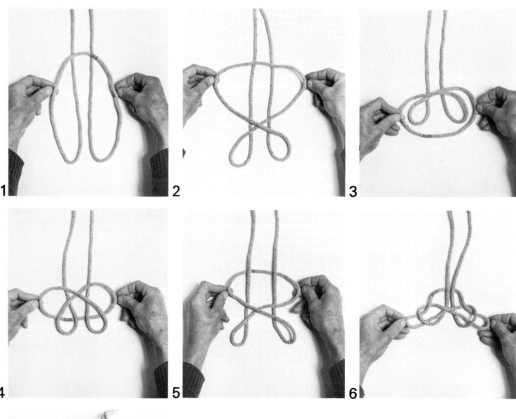

1 2 3

4 5 6

7

Consider the two knots shown in Fig 3. Are they both reef knots? The lower has been called a thief knot, but to avoid confusion with the draw hitch (a fire-service term), also sometimes called a thief knot, perhaps a combination of thief and reef is preferable.

It is a 'tell-tale' knot, which if used to tie the neck of a sea-bag for instance, may not catch a thief but will indicate some interference, as the chances are that the intruder will re-tie the bag with a normal reef knot.

42
'Threef' Knot

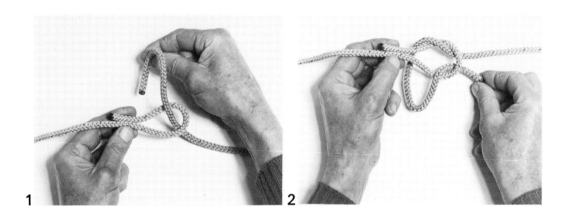

2

1

3

43
Blood Knot

This knot is usually associated with small cordage, particularly if slippery, making it a favourite amongst fishermen for joining nylon lines etc. The knot illustrated is the most common but there are several variations.

Figs 1 to 3 show the right-hand half of the knot, after which the process is repeated with the other end, working in the opposite direction, Figs 4 and 5.

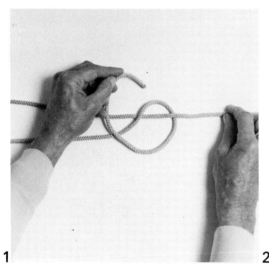

1

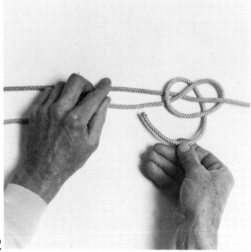

2

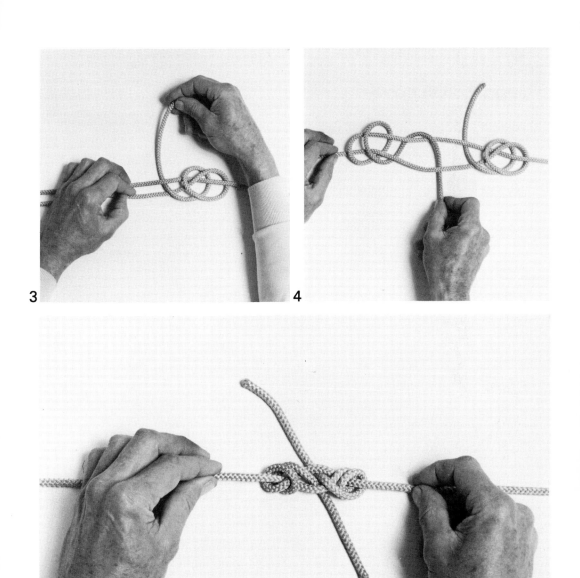

3

4

5

44
Constrictor
Knot

This is an extremely useful working knot for when hauled tight it will lock solid, making it ideal for a quick lashing around, say, a bundle of rods or something similar. It is shown here as an easily applied temporary whipping, saving time, effort and sail twine.

1

2

3

45 Waggoners' Hitch

Habitually used by lorry drivers to lash down loads it is the combination of a knot and a purchase which has been in use for many years as its name implies. The purchase is very similar to a Spanish burton (without blocks), giving a mechanical advantage which allows the standing part to be bowsed-down really tightly. The bight held on the left-hand side, Fig 7, would be around a cleat, the right-hand end providing the hauling part. It comprises half a sheep shank, Figs 1 to 3, with the bight twisted several times, Figs 4 and 5, before the bight of the hauling part is passed through, Fig 6, and arranged ready for hauling, Fig 7.

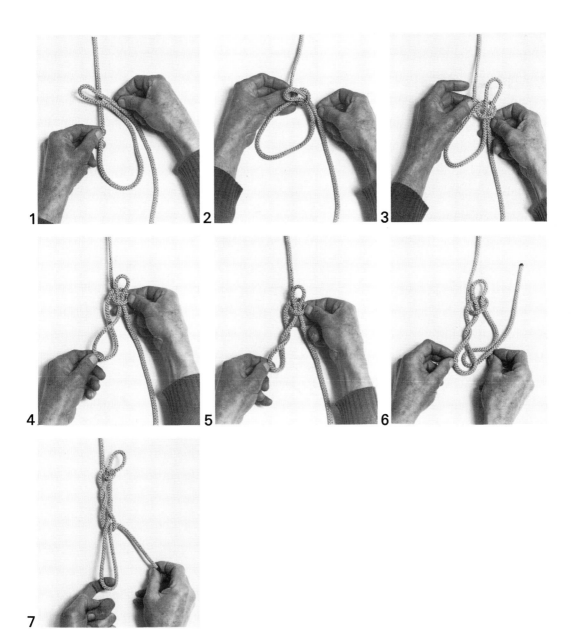

46
Heaving
Line Bend

As the name implies this bend is used to make a heaving line fast to a hawser. It is quickly and easily applied, will not jam and being almost a slippery hitch can equally quickly be 'let go', particularly if the heaving line has a monkey's fist on its end.

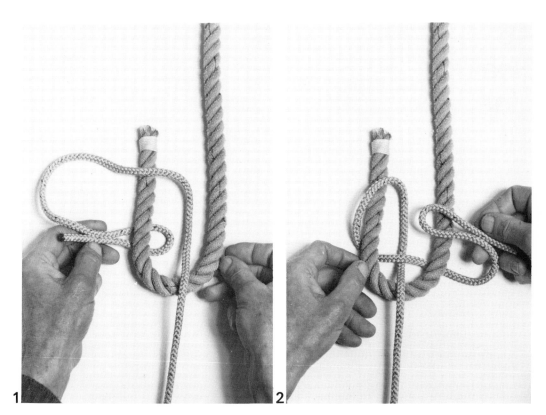

1

2

3

47
Small Bell Toggle, Single Stranded

Although useful on a small bell, this is something of a novelty to illustrate what can be done on a single strand, one end of which stops at the commencement of the square plait, whilst the other continues through to the tassel.

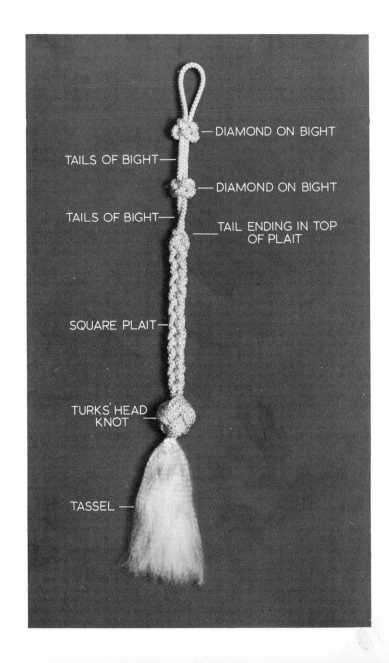

DIAMOND ON BIGHT

TAILS OF BIGHT

DIAMOND ON BIGHT

TAILS OF BIGHT

TAIL ENDING IN TOP OF PLAIT

SQUARE PLAIT

TURKS' HEAD KNOT

TASSEL

This example of a typical bell toggle was made from three lengths of 3mm diameter standard eight strand plait. Two strands being 10ft long and one 9ft, all doubled to form six strands, resulting in the finished toggle being 12in long, including a 4in-long tassel.
It was made without a heart, but a wooden meat skewer forced up through on completion not only tightens the lay but also provides a useful stiffness.

48
Large Bell Toggle, Six Stranded

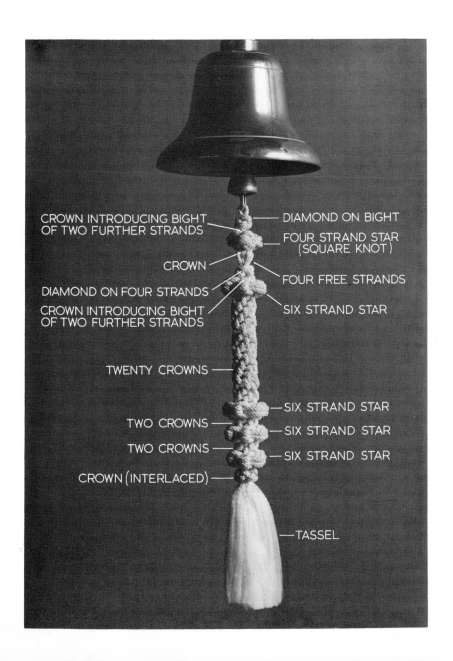

CROWN INTRODUCING BIGHT OF TWO FURTHER STRANDS

CROWN

DIAMOND ON FOUR STRANDS

CROWN INTRODUCING BIGHT OF TWO FURTHER STRANDS

TWENTY CROWNS

TWO CROWNS

TWO CROWNS

CROWN (INTERLACED)

DIAMOND ON BIGHT

FOUR STRAND STAR (SQUARE KNOT)

FOUR FREE STRANDS

SIX STRAND STAR

SIX STRAND STAR

SIX STRAND STAR

SIX STRAND STAR

TASSEL

49
Suggested
Layout of
Multi-Unit
Mat

Mats, perhaps more than any other form of decorative
ropework, provide the means of creating a multitude of
designs, the illustration merely showing a suggested layout
comprising a jury mat centrepiece surrounded by an oval
of double chain plait.
Eleven individual carrick mats surround the centrepiece
followed by four runs of three-strand common sennit,
the first scolloped and the remainder forming the border,
the whole being sewn together with sail twine or the
modern equivalent.

Glossary

Bight A bight is the curvature of a rope when its direction is changed from that of a straight line to the maximum of a full circle.

Bowse-Down The act of hauling tight by means of a purchase, with or without sheave blocks.

Braided/Plaited Rope As distinct from a 'laid' rope, one in which strands are woven, with or without a central core or when a woven core is enclosed within a woven outer sheath.

Hawser A heavy mooring rope.

Heaving Line A light, throwing line, subsequently used to haul a heavier rope ashore.

Lay The word has two definitions when applied to rope. It can mean the direction in which the strands were twisted during the manufacture of the rope, ie, a right- or left-handed 'lay'.
Alternatively, it can mean the 'nature' of the rope when, dependent on how tightly the yarns were twisted during manufacture a rope may have a soft, medium or hard 'lay'.

Lay In decorative work it means the pattern resulting from the assembled strands.

Monkey's Fist A rope ball formed on the end of a heaving line to give it carrying quality.

Parts, relative to Turks' Head The number of strands seen on cross-section if the knot was cut across prior to any 'follow around'. The number of parts governs the length of the knot.

Purchase An arrangement of rope, with or without sheave blocks, whereby a mechanical advantage is obtained.

Quid Slang term for the British one pound note or the older golden coin, the sovereign.

Serving Without becoming involved with worming and parcelling which apply more to working knots and splices, *serving* means being wrapped around tightly with some form of cordage. See Knot 9.

Standing Part The remaining part of a rope other than the 'hauling' part, the ends, a bight or that amount used in making a knot, usually that part which is under load.

Strands Laid yarns. The appropriate number of strands being laid together to form the finished rope.

Tack The lower, forward corner of a fore and aft sail.

Tail or Tail End The extreme end of a rope or any of its individual strands.

Topping Lift Part of the running rigging from the mast to the outer end of a boom to relieve the sail from the weight of the latter, usually associated with older vessels. Set in pairs, one each side of the sail.

Turns, relative to a Turk's Head The number of 'cross-overs' made before the working end returns to meet the standing part, in parallel, for the first time. The diameter of the cylinder, in relation to the diameter of the cordage used, governs the number of turns required.

Whipping A series of turns of sail twine or similar, forming a lashing at the end of a rope or any of its individual strands to prevent fraying.

Yarns Woven fibres laid up together.